This book is for:

ONE WHO FOLLOWS
HARD AFTER GOD.
MAY YOU CATCH HIM
AND BE CAUGHT
BY HIM.

THE
HEART OF A
GOD CHASER

TOMMY TENNEY

THE
HEART OF A
GOD
CHASER

TOMMY TENNEY

ALBURY PUBLISHING
TULSA, OKLAHOMA

Second Printing

The Heart of a God Chaser
ISBN 1-57778-187-2
Copyright ©2000 by Tommy Tenney

Published by ALBURY PUBLISHING
P. O. Box 470406
Tulsa, Oklahoma 74147-0406

Introduction

Throughout history there have been God chasers—
men and women whose passion and love for God led
them to great truths and insights into who God is.
Many of them left behind a trail for us to follow
through their teachings and writings, with the ultimate
hope that we would go beyond words on a page and
take up the pursuit ourselves. People like A. W. Tozer,
John Wesley, Madame Guyon, Andrew Murray, and
others offer a legacy of knowing and loving God that
inspires present-day believers to cease seeking God's
hands and instead to seek His face.

The purpose of the quotes, hymns, scriptures, and poems selected for *The Heart of a God Chaser* is to spur you on in your quest for God. The inspirations penned by God chasers, past and present, will refresh, renew, and refuel your heart's desire to know Him, to see His face.

Being a God chaser is not pursuing knowledge about God; it is knowing God in an intimate, intensely personal way. It is to chase after God until you apprehend His glory. Don't stop short. Don't give up. God is just waiting to be "caught" by you!

WHAT IS A *God* CHASER?

A God chaser is

an individual

whose hunger

exceeds his reach.

—Tommy Tenney

PURSUING

Your worship must

engage your spirit

in the pursuit of truth.

—*John 4:23* THE MESSAGE

As a God chaser, I resolve not to fight against the inner turmoil and desperately strive to resolve it, but to accept it and relax into it, recognizing it as a desire and hunger for more of God. This drive accompanies me in every task, but never hazes my focus on the matter at hand. It actually intensifies and sharpens my focus when I seek to see God in, please God with, and serve God in everything I do.

—*Tommy Tenney*

DIVINE
Resolution

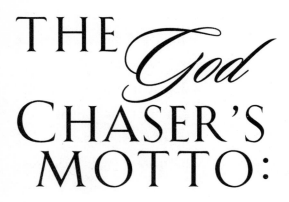

THE *God* CHASER'S MOTTO:

Self-abandonment to

divine providence.

—*Jean Pierrre de Caussade*

All the time we are pursuing

Him we are already in His hand.

THE

Paradoxical

PURSUIT

—*A. W. Tozer*

DIVINE *Tag*

Catching Him. Really, it's an impossible phrase. We can no more catch Him than the east can catch the west; they're too far removed from each other. It's like playing chase with my daughter. I really don't have to run. I just artfully dodge this way and then that, and she can't even touch me, because a six-year-old can't catch an adult. But that's really not the purpose of the game, because a few minutes into it, she laughingly says, "Oh, Daddy," and it's at that moment that she captures my heart, if not my presence or body. And then I turn and she's no longer chasing me, but I'm chasing her, and I catch her and we tumble in the grass with hugs and kisses. The pursuer becomes the pursued.

—*Tommy Tenney*

MY SOUL
Desire

O grant that nothing in my soul

May dwell, but Thy pure love alone!

O may thy love possess me whole.

My joy, my treasure, and my crown.

Strange flames far from my heart remove!

My every act, word, thought, be love.

—*John Wesley*

ALL-*Consuming* FIRE

The fire of God, as it comes to
purify, to consume the sacrifice and
convert it into its own heavenly
light-nature, to baptize with the
Holy Ghost and with fire, to
transform our being into flames of
love—blessed is the man who
knows His God as a consuming fire.
—*Andrew Murray*

God IS NOW

Perhaps the masses of people are

happy to know where God's been,

but true God chasers are not

content just to study God's trail,

His truths; they want to know Him.

They want to know where He is

and what He's doing right now.

—*Tommy Tenney*

My soul followeth hard after thee.

—Psalm 63:8 KJV

THE
PSALMIST
David,
GOD
CHASER

PURSUING
Pilgrims

He who would valiant be 'gainst all disaster,

Let him in constancy follow the Master.

There's no discouragement shall make him

    once relent

His first avowed intent to be a pilgrim.

Since, LORD, Thou dost defend us with Thy

    Spirit,

We know we at the end shall life inherit.

Then fancies flee away! I'll fear not what men say,

I'll labor night and day to be a pilgrim.

—*John Bunyan*

DEAD MAN
Walking

Only dead men see God's face, so
when you go behind that veil you
have to say, "I'm really not alive
anymore. I'm a walking dead
man.". . . That is how a Christian
lives out Romans 12:1—dead man
walking.

—*Tommy Tenney*

A
PERSONAL
Quest

We need our God; He is to

be had for the seeking; and

He will not deny Himself

to any one of us if we

personally seek His face.

—*Charles H. Spurgeon*

A BASIC
Requirement

Humiliation is the beginning of sanctification;

and as without this, without holiness, no man

shall see God, though he pore whole nights upon

his Bible; so without that, without humility, no

man shall hear God speak to his soul, though he

hear three, two-hour sermons every day.

—*John Donne*

God doesn't really care about

anything you can do for

Him; He only cares about

your answer to one question:

Do you want Me?

—*Tommy Tenney*

Desire

By the quality of our inner lives I do not
mean something characterized by ferocious
intensity and strain. I mean rather such a
humble and genial devotedness as we find in
the most loving of the saints. I mean the
quality which makes contagious Christians,
makes people catch the love of God from you.

—*Evelyn Underhill*

Contagious

CHASERS

THE RIGHT
Appetite

Blessed are they which

do hunger and thirst

after righteousness: for

they shall be filled.

—*Matthew 5:6* KJV

WHO IS *Chasing* WHOM?

We pursue God because,

and only because, He has

first put an urge within us

that spurs us to the pursuit.

—*A. W. Tozer*

THE WAY Back Home

Repentance prepares us for
His presence. In fact, you
cannot live in His presence
without repentance.
Repentance permits
pursuit of His presence.
It builds the road for
you to get to God
(or for God to get to you!).

—*Tommy Tenney*

[Accustom] yourself then by degrees thus to worship Him, to beg His grace, to offer Him your heart from time to time, in the midst of your business, even every moment if you can. Do not always scrupulously confine yourself to certain rules, or particular forms of devotion; but act with a general confidence in God, with love and humility.

—*Brother Lawrence*

Moment
BY Moment

God's
WORK

The great work of God in heaven,

the chief thought and longing of

His heart is, in His Son, to reach

your heart and speak to you.

—Andrew Murray

Nearer TO THEE

Nearer, my God, to thee, nearer to thee!

E'en though it be a cross that raiseth me,

Still all my song shall be,

Nearer, my God, to thee;

Nearer, my God, to thee, nearer to thee!

Though like the wanderer.

The sun gone down,

Darkness be over me, my rest a stone;

Yet in my dreams I'd be

Nearer, my God, to thee;

Nearer, my God, to thee, nearer to thee!

Of it, on joyful wing cleaving the sky,

Sun, moon, and stars forgot, upward I fly,

Still all my song shall be,

Nearer, my God, to thee;

Nearer, my God, to thee, nearer to thee!

—*Sarah F. Adams*

VALUED
BY *God*

This is the one I esteem:

he who is humble and

contrite in spirit, and

trembles at my word.

—*Isaiah 66:2*

Justice and Judgment are thy throne

Yet wondrous is thy grace;

While truth and mercy joined in one,

Invite us near thy face.

—*Isaac Watts*

There is much more of God available than we have ever known or imagined, but we have become so satisfied with where we are and what we have that we don't press in for God's best. Yes, God is moving among us and working in our lives, but we have been content to comb the carpet for crumbs as opposed to having the abundant loaves of hot bread God has prepared for us in the ovens of heaven! He has prepared a great table of His presence in this day, and He is calling to the Church, "Come and dine."

—*Tommy Tenney*

Fresh
BREAD

BETTER
THAN I
Know
MYSELF

God interposes Himself, as it were,
between me and myself; He separates me
from myself; He desires to be nearer to
me by His pure love than I am to myself.
He would have me look upon this "me" as
a stranger; He would have me escape from
its walls, sacrifice it whole to Him,
returning it absolutely and unconditionally
to Him from whom I received it.

—*François Fénelon*

Ransomed man need no longer

pause in fear to enter the Holy of

Holies. God wills that we should

push on into His presence and

live our whole life there.

—*A. W. Tozer*

Come

AND *Stay*

Dear Christian friends, I plead with you to give your bodies to God. Let them be a living and holy sacrifice—the kind he will accept. When you think of what he has done for you, is this too much to ask?

—*Romans 12:1* NLT

A SMALL Price

God's
DESIRE

Though you may think yourself ever so

dull and incapable of sublime attainments,

yet by prayer the possession and

enjoyment of God is easily obtained; for

He is more desirous to give Himself to us

than we can be to receive Him.

—*William Backhouse and James Janson*

CATCHING
THE *Catcher*

He will not frustrate us. God will allow Himself to be caught by us. As a father playing tag with his child allows himself to be caught by the laughing, loving child, so too will the heavenly Father allow Himself to be caught. In fact, just when we would tire in despair, He will turn and catch us. He wants to be "captured" by our love. He eagerly awaits the laughing, loving encounter. He has missed those times with man since the Garden. Intuitively, God chasers have known this. They were willing to chase the "uncatchable," knowing the "impossible" would catch them.

—*Tommy Tenney*

Breaking
THROUGH
THE CLOUD

Peace comes when there is no cloud
between us and God. Peace is the
consequence of forgiveness, God's
removal of that which obscures His
face and so breaks union with Him.
The happy sequence culminating in
fellowship with God is penitence,
pardon, and peace—the first we
offer, the second we accept, and the
third we inherit.

—_Charles H. Brent_

AMAZING

Grace

God is none other than the Saviour of our

wretchedness. So we can only know God

well by knowing our iniquities. . . . Those

who have known God without knowing

their wretchedness have not glorified

Him, but have glorified themselves.

—*Blaise Pascal*

THE *Best* CHOICE

Thou hidden love of God, whose height,

Whose depth unfathomed no one knows

I see from far thy beauteous light,

And inly sigh for thy repose;

My heart is pained, nor can it be

At rest, till it finds rest in thee.

O Love, thy sovereign aid impart

To save me from low-thoughted care;

Chase this self-will from all my heart,

From all its hidden mazes there;

Make me thy duteous child that I

Ceaseless may "Abba, Father" cry.

Each moment draw from earth away

My heart that lowly waits thy call;

Speak to my inmost soul and say

"I am thy love, thy God, thy all!"

To feel thy power, to hear thy voice,

To taste thy love, be all my choice.

—*Gerhard Tersteegen, translated by John Wesley*

Then Moses said, "I pray that you will let me see you in all of your glory." The LORD answered: All right. I am the LORD, and I show mercy and kindness to anyone I choose. I will let you see my glory and hear my holy name.

—Exodus 33:18-19 CEV

THE
DELIVERER
Moses,
GOD
CHASER

God is everywhere, but He doesn't turn His face and His favor everywhere. That is why He tells us to seek His face. Yes, He is present with you every time you meet with other believers in a worship service, but how long has it been since your hunger caused you to crawl up in His lap, and like a child, to reach up and take the face of God to turn it toward you? Intimacy with Him! That is what God desires, and His face should be our highest focus.

—*Tommy Tenney*

OUR *Highest* FOCUS

ALONE IN THE *Crowd*

Brethren, when we finally have
our meeting with God, it has to
be alone in the depths of our
being. We will be alone even if
we are surrounded by a crowd.
God has to cut every maverick
out of the herd and brand him
all alone. It isn't something that
God can do for us *en masse*.

—*A. W. Tozer*

GET A *Clue*

God has set this whole thing up
so that we cannot truly know
who we are and how we are to
operate except by coming to
Him and hearing it straight from
Him. It is imperative for us to
fellowship with the Father to
understand Him, to understand
ourselves, and to comprehend
His plan for us. Without intimacy
with Him, we are clueless!

—*Tommy Tenney*

Godly
ADVICE

He is no fool who gives

what he cannot keep to

gain what he cannot lose.

—*Jim Elliot*

And he said unto him, If thy presence go not with me, carry us not up hence.

—Exodus 33:15 KJV

"If You're not going, I'm not going!" Rings true, doesn't it? "Where You go, I will go." Sound familiar? It's the mantra of men and women on a mission: the pursuit of His presence. "LORD, if You don't go, don't expect me to go. I'm staying with You. I'm only happy in Your presence." Let this God chaser become a God catcher.

—*Tommy Tenney*

Side
BY *Side*

TRUE *Life*

God—you're my God! I can't get enough of you! I've worked up such hunger and thirst for God, traveling across dry and weary deserts. So here I am in the place of worship, eyes open, drinking in your strength and glory. In your generous love I am really living at last! My lips brim praises like fountains. I bless you every time I take a breath; My arms wave like banners of praise to you.

—*Psalm 63:1-4* THE MESSAGE

IT'S
NOT WHAT
You
KNOW

God's voice is not asking what you
know, but "Are you willing? Will you
yield your life to Me? Will you give up
the things of this world—the weights
and the anchors of this world that hold
you down—and come away with Me?
Come into the spirit realm that I have
made for you. I will carry you and show
you the glory I have waiting for you."

—*Roberts Liardon*

"Let all the angels of God worship Him." All the servants around His throne point to Him: it is to Him we must look. And that in worship. It is worship, worship, worship the Son must have. It is to the heart that worships Him He will make Himself known.

—*Andrew Murray*

We all should be willing to work for the LORD, but it is a matter of grace on God's part. I am of the opinion that we should not be concerned about working for God until we have learned the meaning and the delight of worshiping Him. A worshiper can work with eternal quality in his work. But a worker who does not worship is only piling up wood, hay, and stubble for the time when God sets the world on fire.

—*A. W. Tozer*

Worshiper FIRST, WORKER SECOND

Determination

God is looking for someone who is willing to tie a rope around an ankle and say, "If I perish, I perish; but I am going to see the King. I want to do everything I can to go behind that veil. I'm going to put on the blood, I'm going to repent, I'm going to do everything I can because I'm tired of knowing about Him. I want to know Him. I've got to see His face."

—*Tommy Tenney*

TEMPLES
OF *Fire*

If, when the people obeyed, the
glory of God came down and the
people fall prostrate, how much
glory ought there to be today? . . .
The ancient temple in all its glory
represents each one of our bodies.
If we are filled with the Holy
Ghost, as we ought to be, the
body will be flooded with rivers
of water flowing out to others;
and it will be on fire for God.

—*Maria Woodworth Etter*

Let us run with perseverance
the race marked out for us.
Let us fix our eyes on Jesus,
the author and perfecter of
our faith....Consider him who
endured such opposition from
sinful men, so that you will
not grow weary and lose heart.
—*Hebrews 12:1-3* NIV

FIX
OUR
Eyes
ON
Jesus

BROKEN AND *Spilled* OUT

Did you notice that God didn't break Mary's alabaster box? Mary had to break it. If you want to have that kind of encounter with God, then you will have to "break" yourself. The highest level of worship comes from brokenness.

—*Tommy Tenney*

(See Mark 14:3.)

DRAW ME Nearer

I am thine, O LORD, I have heard thy voice,

And it told thy love to me;

But I long to rise in the arms of faith

And be closer drawn to thee

Draw me nearer, nearer, blessed LORD,

To the cross where thou hast died.

Draw me nearer, nearer, nearer, blessed LORD,

To thy precious, bleeding side.

Consecrate me now to thy service, LORD,

By the power of grace divine;

Let my soul look up with a steadfast hope,

And my will be lost in thine.

O the pure delight of a single hour

That before thy throne I spend,

When I kneel in prayer, and with thee, my God,

I commune as friend with friend!

—*Fannie J. Crosby*

WHEN ISAIAH *Caught* GOD

Then said I, Woe is me!
For I am undone;
because I am a man of
unclean lips, and I dwell
in the midst of a people
of unclean lips: for mine
eyes have seen the King,
the LORD of hosts.

—Isaiah 6:5 KJV

God doesn't want us to turn away from His glory so we can build pitiful monuments to a momentary revelation we never paid for with our tears. Salvation is a free gift, but God's glory will cost us everything. He wants us to press in and live in His perpetual habitation of glory. He wants us to be so saturated with His presence and glory that we carry His presence with us everywhere we go in this life.

—*Tommy Tenney*

THE *Glorious* COST

THE *Only* WAY

There is only one way to love God,

that is not to take one step without

Him and to follow with a brave

heart wherever He leads.

—*François Fénelon*

The LORD is close to the

brokenhearted and saves those

who are crushed in spirit.

—*Psalm 34:18*

Something

always dies when

God's glory

encounters living

flesh.

—*Tommy Tenney*

Death
TO SELF

THIS
WAY, *Please*

We want to reach the kingdom

of God, but we don't want to

travel by way of death. And

yet there stands Necessity

saying: "This way, please."

Do you hesitate, man, to go

this way, when this is the

way that God came to you?

—*Saint Augustine*

Sleeping AND WAKING

Keep us, LORD, so awake in the duties

of our callings that we may sleep in

thy peace and wake in thy glory.

—John Donne

God is sheer being itself—

Spirit. Those who worship

him must do it out of their

very being, their spirits, their

true selves, in adoration.

—*John 4:24* THE MESSAGE

The spiritual giants of old were men who at some time became acutely conscious of the real Presence of God and maintained that consciousness for the rest of their lives. The first encounter may have been one of terror, as when a "horror of great darkness" fell upon Abram. . . Usually this fear soon lost its content of terror and changed after a while to delightsome awe, to level off finally into a reverent sense of complete nearness to God. The essential point is, they experienced God.

—*A. W. Tozer*

THE *Bare* ESSENTIALS

Vain
IMAGINATIONS

Do you really think God needs us to do

things for Him? Isn't He the Creator who

stepped out on the balcony of heaven and

scooped out the seven seas with the palms

of His hands? Wasn't it God who pinched

the earth to make the mountains? Then

obviously He doesn't need you to "do"

anything. What He wants is your worship.

—*Tommy Tenney*

Pray WITHOUT Ceasing

He prays well

who is so absorbed

with God that he

does not know he

is praying.

—*Francis de Sales*

THE

LORD, help us to know that our God is the same forever. God would ever dwell with His people. He does not want to live apart from them. His delight and pleasure is to ever be with them. He would walk with them; and wherever the footsteps of God have been among His people, He has left a beautiful pathway of light and glory. God delights to reveal His arm of power; He rejoices to show forth His glory. He "maketh a way in the sea, and a path in the mighty waters" (Isaiah 43:16 KJV).

—*Maria Woodworth Etter*

Illumination

For God, who said, "Let

light shine out of

darkness," made his light

shine in our hearts to give

us the light of the

knowledge of the glory of

God in the face of Christ.

—2 Corinthians 4:6

FROM *Glory*
TO *Glory*

Every experience with God is terrific and

life-changing, but we cannot live from one

experience to the next. To keep the edge

we must go from glory to glory, and that

means every day we are spending time

with God and letting Him change us and

direct us. If we have a profound, life-

changing experience, that's great! But what

we live for is simply living in the presence

of God and following after Jesus.

—*Ron Luce*

ASK Rightly

Picture God as saying to you, "My son, why is it that day by day you rise, and pray, and even strike the ground with your forehead, nay sometimes even shed tears, while you say to Me: 'My Father, give me wealth!' If I were to give it to you, you would think yourself of some importance, you would fancy that you had gained something very great. Because you asked for it, you have it. But take care to make good use of it. Before you had it, you were humble; now that you have begun to be rich, you despise the poor."
—*St. Augustine*

THE ELEMENTS OF *Prayer*

Its ground: God, by whose goodness

it springeth in us.

Its use: to turn our will to His will.

Its end: to be made one with Him

and like to Him in all things.

—*Julian of Norwich*

As well might a gnat seek to

drink in the ocean, as a finite

creature to comprehend the

Eternal God.

—*Charles H. Spurgeon*

Get clear hold of the three elements of

success in a race: self-denial, that gives

up everything that hinders; decision,

that puts the whole heart into the work

and runs; patience, that day by day

afresh enters the course.

Run —*Andrew Murray*

TO WIN

Not that I have already obtained

all this, or have already been

made perfect, but I press on to

take hold of that for which

Christ Jesus took hold of me.

—*Philippians 3:12*

THE
APOSTLE
Paul,
GOD
CHASER

ALL *Creation* DECLARES

It is not with a doubtful consciousness, but one fully certain that I love thee, O LORD. Thou hast smitten my heart with thy Word, and I have loved thee. And see also the heaven, and earth, and all that is in them—on every side they tell me to love thee, and they do not cease to tell this to all men, "so that they are without excuse."

—*Saint Augustine*

THE *Scent*
OF DEATH

The more death that God smells, the
closer He can come. It's as if the smell of
that sacrifice was a signal that God could
draw near to His people for a moment
without striking them down for their sin.
His end goal has always been reunion and
intimate communion with mankind, His
highest creation, but sin made that a fatal
affair. God cannot come close to living
flesh because it reeks of the world. It has
to be dead flesh for Him to come close.

—*Tommy Tenney*

The most perfect way of seeking God, and
the most suitable order, is not for us to
attempt with bold curiosity to penetrate to
the investigation of His essence, which we
ought more to adore than meticulously to
search out, but for us to contemplate Him
in His works, whereby He renders Himself
near and familiar to us, and in some
manner communicates Himself.

—*John Calvin*

Perfect
SEEKING

A CHASER'S *Prayer* FOR *Grace*

O Lord our God, grant us grace to desire

Thee with our whole heart; that, so

desiring, we may seek, and seeking find

Thee; and so finding Thee may love Thee;

and loving Thee, may hate those sins from

which Thou hast redeemed us.

—*Saint Anselm*

WE CRY,
"*Abba*"

We must put away all

effort to impress and

come with the guileless

candor of childhood.

—*A. W. Tozer*

The high and lofty one who inhabits eternity, the Holy One, says this: "I live in that high and holy place with those whose spirits are contrite and humble. I refresh the humble and give new courage to those with repentant hearts."

HIGH AND *Holy*

—*Isaiah 57:15* NLT

Once you experience God in His glory, you can't turn away from Him or forget His touch. It's not just as argument of a doctrine; it's an experience. That is why the apostle Paul said, " I know whom I have believed" (2 Timothy 1:12). Unfortunately, many people in the Church would say, "I know *about* whom I have believed." That means they haven't met Him in His glory.

—*Tommy Tenney*

Old things are passed away.

Let worldly minds the world pursue,

It has no charms for me;

Once I admired its trifles too,

But grace has set me free.

I SEE THE *Lord*

Its pleasures now no longer please,

No more content afford;

Far from my heart be joys like these;

Now I have seen the LORD.

As by the light of op'ning day

The stars are all concealed;

So earthly pleasures fade away,

When Jesus is revealed.

—John Newton

Happy is the man who gives himself to

God! Happy are they who throw

themselves with bowed head and closed

eyes into the arms of the "Father of mercies"

and the "God of all consolation."

—*François Fénelon*

REAL *Happiness*

A *Desirable* SACRIFICE

The sacrifice you want

is a broken spirit. A

broken and repentant

heart, O God,

you will not despise.

—*Psalm 51:17* NLT

Digging THE WELL

I encourage you to linger and soak in the presence of the LORD at every opportunity. When you draw near to Him, don't hurry and don't rush. Realize that this is (or should be) at the top of your priority list. Let God do a deep work in your heart and life. This is the way God creates a "deep-bored" well in your life that will become an artesian well of power and glory in His presence. The purpose of His presence is to bring deliverance to the captives and victory to the children.

—*Tommy Tenney*

Why is it that people are slow to yield themselves to the control and government and guidance of the Spirit of God? Why is it that there is not a divine passion in our hearts that such a blessed control should be made a possibility? Shall you and I today assert our own little humanity and walk according to our own light, or shall we as wise men, as those who seek the divinest in life, say yes to God and let God take our being, inhabit our being, and let Him live His life in us, and then He will manifest His life through us?

—*John G. Lake*

A PRESSING *Question*

What kind of a good is that which only makes you worse? For worse you are, since you were bad already. And that it would make you worse you knew not; hence you asked it of Me. I gave it to you, and I proved you; you have found—and you have found out! Ask of Me better things than these, greater things than these. Ask of Me spiritual things. Ask of Me Myself!

—*Saint Augustine*

Asking

RIGHTLY

SECRET
Communion

For the first two or three years after my
conversion, I used to ask for specific things.
Now I ask for God. . . [I]f God is your
own, then all things in heaven and on earth
will be your own, because He is your Father
and is everything to you; otherwise you will
have to go and ask like a beggar for certain
things. When they are used up, you will
have to ask again. So ask not for gifts but
for the Giver of Gifts: not for life but for
the Giver of Life—then life and the things
needed for life will be added unto you.

—*Sadhu Sundar Singh*

LET ME *Burn*

If you are hungry for the fire to fall in your church, then you need to just crawl up on the altar and say, "God, whatever it takes. I lay myself on the altar and ask You to consume me with Your fire, LORD." Then we can follow the lead of John Wesley, who explained how he drew such large crowds during the First Great Awakening: "I set myself on fire, and the people come to see me burn."

—*Tommy Tenney*

"Abraham believed God, and it was credited to him as righteousness," and he was called God's friend.

—James 2:23

THE
PATRIARCH
Abraham,
GOD
CHASER

Open
THE WINDOWS

God has a special way of

satisfying the cry of His children.

He is waiting to open to us the

windows of heaven until He has

so moved in the depths of our

heart that everything unlike

Himself has been destroyed.

—*Smith Wigglesworth*

Holy STILLNESS

Deep restfulness, even amid outward

activity, is one of the most beautiful

marks and aids of the life of faith.

Cultivate that holy stillness that seeks to

abide in God's presence and does not

yield too much to things around.

—*Andrew Murray*

Seeker

I sought Him where my logic led.
"This friend is always sure and right;
His lantern is sufficient light—I need
no star," I said.

I sought Him in the city square.
Logic and I went up and down
The marketplace of many a town,
And He was never there.

I tracked Him to the mind's far rim.
The valiant Intellect went forth
To east and west and south and north,
And found no trace of Him.

We walked the world from sun to sun,
Logic and I, with little Faith,
But never came to Nazareth,
Or found the Holy One.

I sought in vain. And finally,
Back to the heart's small house I crept,
And fell upon my knees, and wept;
And lo!—He came to me!
—*Sara Henderson Hay*

The apostle Paul said, "But none of these things move me, neither count I my life dear unto myself, so that I might finish my course with joy, and the ministry, which I have received of the LORD Jesus, to testify the gospel of the grace of God" (Acts 20:24). This is the confession of people in love and in intimate communion with their Maker.

—*Tommy Tenney*

A CHASER'S
Confession

ETERNAL *Senses*

What hinders men from seeing and hearing God is their own hearing, seeing, and willing; by their own wills they separate themselves from the will of God. They see and hear within their own desires, which obstructs them from seeing and hearing God. Terrestrial and material things overshadow them, and they cannot see beyond their own human nature. If they would be still, desist from thinking and feeling with their own self-hood, subdue the self-will, enter into a state of resignation, into a divine union with Christ, who sees God, and hears God, and speaks with him, who knows the word and will of God; then would the eternal hearing, seeing, and speaking become revealed to them.

—*Jacob Boehme*

THE *Edge*

Separate yourself from the crowd and go into the Holy of Holies. Ask the LORD to show you what is preventing you from having the edge and repent. Cry out to Him and say, "God, I'm going for the gold. I want the Holy of Holies. I want what Elijah had. I want what David had. I want what Moses had. I want what Jacob had when he said, "Give me that blessing!" I want what John the Baptist had. I want what Peter and Paul had. I want the edge, God!"

—*Ron Luce*

Welcome
INVASION

God is tired of having long-distance

relationships with His people. He was tired

of it thousands of years ago in Moses' day,

and He is tired of it today. He really wants

to have intimate, close encounters with you

and me. He wants to invade our homes

with His abiding presence in a way that will

make every visitor begin to weep with

wonder and worship the moment they enter.

—*Tommy Tenney*

I tell you the truth, unless a kernel of

wheat falls to the ground and dies, it

remains only a single seed. But if it

dies, it produces many seeds. The

man who loves his life will lose it,

while the man who hates his life in

this world will keep it for eternal life.

—*John 12:24-25*

WHAT IS *Worship?*

To worship is to quicken the

conscience by the holiness of God,

to purge the imagination by the

beauty of God, to open the heart

to the love of God, and to devote

the will to the purpose of God.

—*William Temple*

Pray Him to
give you
what the
Scriptures
call
"an

YOUR
BEST
Heart

honest and good heart" or "a perfect
heart;" and, without waiting, begin at
once to obey Him with the best heart you
have. Any obedience is better than none.
You have to seek His face; obedience is
the only way of seeing Him. All your
duties are obediences. To do what He bids
is to obey Him, and to obey Him is to
approach Him. Every act of obedience is
an approach—an approach to Him who
is not far off, though He seems so, but
close behind this visible screen of things
hiding Him from us.

—*John Henry Newman*

THE *Still Small* VOICE

Retire from the world each day to some private spot. . . . Stay in the secret place till the surrounding noises begin to fade out of your heart and a sense of God's presence envelops you. Deliberately tune out the unpleasant sounds and come out of your closet determined not to hear them. Listen for the inward voice till you learn to recognize it.

—*A. W. Tozer*

LORD, put a hunger in our

hearts for You and not just

for Your things. We

appreciate Your boundless

blessings, Father, but we are

hungry for You, our Blesser.

Come show us the real

purpose of Your presence.

—*Tommy Tenney*

THE WEIGHT OF HIS Glory

And it came to pass, when the priests were come out of the holy place, that the cloud filled the house of the LORD, so that the priests could not stand to minister because of the cloud: for the glory of the LORD had filled the house of the LORD.

—1 Kings 8:10-11 KJV

What He wants us to do is just look at Him. Yes, we can tell Him what we feel. We need to tell Him, but He is really waiting to receive our most intimate worship and adoration, the kind that transcends mere words or outward actions.

He has set before you an open door, but you will have to "face" Him. You cannot back your way into the door of eternity; you have to walk into it.

—*Tommy Tenney*

WORDS CANNOT Express

The blessed and inviting truth

is that God is the most

winsome of all beings, and in

our worship of Him we should

find unspeakable pleasure.

—*A. W. Tozer*

PRAYER
OF THE
Day

Father, we thank You for Your
presence. LORD, the air is just
pregnant with possibility and we
sense Your nearness. But we
must say that You are not near
enough. Come, Holy Spirit. If
not now, when? If not us, to
whom? And if not here, where?
Just tell us, LORD, and we'll go;
we will pursue Your presence
because we want You, LORD.
Your presence is what we are
after and nothing less will do.

—*Tommy Tenney*

Constantly practice the habit of inwardly gazing upon God. You know that something inside your heart sees God. Even when you are compelled to withdraw your conscious attention in order to engage in earthly affairs, there is within you a secret communion always going on.

—*A. W. Tozer*

SECRET
Communion

God will whisper His prophetic secrets before they ever come to pass for broken-box worshipers and fragrant anointers. He will turn aside at the height of His glory for people who will dismantle their own glory and ego just to share His shame as their own.

—*Tommy Tenney*

FRAGRANT *Followers*

The LORD said to him [Solomon]: "I have heard the prayer and plea you have made before me; I have consecrated this temple, which you have built, by putting my Name there forever. My eyes and my heart will always be there."

—*1 Kings 9:3*

THE TEMPLE BUILDER

Solomon, GOD CHASER

God is our true Friend, who
always gives us the counsel and
comfort we need. Our danger
lies in resisting Him; so it is
essential that we acquire the
habit of hearkening to His
voice, or keeping silence within,
and listening so as to lose
nothing of what He says to us.

—*François Fénelon*

God, as the author of our being, longs to have us yield ourselves and wait upon Himself to work His work in us. As the righteous and holy One, He seeks to have us wholly given up to His will and wisdom. As the unseen and hidden One, He asks that we should withdraw ourselves from the visible and hold fellowship with Him. Man was created for the presence of God.

—Andrew Murray

MAN'S *Purpose*

Dearly beloved, whoever you are

who sincerely wish to give yourselves

up to God, I conjure you, that after

having once made the donation, you

take not yourselves back again;

remember, a gift once presented is

no longer at the disposal of the giver.

—*Madame Jeanne Guyon*

It isn't impertinent

to pursue God for

His own sake; it is

God's greatest

desire and delight.

—*Tommy Tenney*

God

WILL RESPOND

The nations will fear the name of

the LORD, all the kings of the earth

will revere your glory. For the

LORD will rebuild Zion and appear

in his glory. He will respond to the

prayer of the destitute; he will not

despise their plea.

—Psalm 102:15-17

WHAT GETS *God's* ATTENTION?

If you want to know why some churches
have revival, or why some people have
intimacy when multitudes do not, the
answer is that these are people of
brokenness. The breaking of your heart
arrests the ears and eyes of God, and it
begins when your love for Him supersedes
your fear of what others may think. You
can't seek His face and save your "face."
The "end" of your glory, the dismantling,
if you please, is the beginning of His glory.

—*Tommy Tenney*

HEAR *God*
WHISPER

Have you ever wondered how certain people
seem to have a certain attachment to God?
For some reason, God just seems to be near
them all the time. I can tell you that it isn't
because they preach so well or because they
are such stellar singers. No, they know how
to dismantle their egos and glory. They lay it
all aside just to worship at His feet in
brokenness and humility. And it is for these
precious few that God Himself will stop His
ascent to heaven just to whisper His secrets
into their waiting hearts.

—*Tommy Tenney*

THE SOURCE OF *Knowledge*

This is what the LORD says, he

who made the earth, the LORD

who formed it and established

it—the LORD is his name: "Call

to me and I will answer you and

tell you great and unsearchable

things you do not know."

—*Jeremiah 33:2-3*

PSALM OF A *God* CHASER

Early, my God, without delay,
I haste to seek thy face;
My thirsty spirit faints away
Without thy cheering grace.

So pilgrims on the scorching sand,
Beneath a burning sky,
Long for a cooling stream at hand,
And they must drink or die.

I've seen thy glory and thy power
Through all thy temple shine;
My God, repeat that heav'nly hour,
That vision so divine.

Not all the blessings of a feast
Can please my soul so well,
As when thy richer grace I taste,
And in thy presence dwell.
—*Isaac Watts, Psalm 63*

He who makes God's glory the

one and only aim before which all

other things bow themselves is the

man to bring honor to his LORD.

—*Charles H. Spurgeon*

Glory in his holy name; let the

hearts of those who seek the LORD

rejoice. Look to the LORD and his

strength; seek his face always.

—*1 Chronicles 16:10-11*

TO KNOW AND BE *Known*

It seems to me, as time goes on,

that the only thing that is worth

seeking for is to know and to be

known by Christ—a privilege

open alone to the childlike, who,

with receptivity, guilelessness,

and humility, move Godward.

—*Charles H. Brent*

"You can't get there from here." So I've been told. Then I must build a road— a highway, a road of repentance! Then I can "get there!" Where is there? In His presence. . . . Build the road of repentance and you get the "King's Highway"— a passageway of His presence to your person.

—*Tommy Tenney*

TRUE
Repentance

Sooner or later repentance must
have a broken and a contrite
heart; we must with our blessed
LORD go over the brook
Cedron, and with Him sweat
great drops of sorrow before He
can say for us, as He said for
Himself: "It is finished."

—*William Law*

Love the LORD

your God with all

your heart and with

all your soul and

with all your mind.

—*Matthew 22:37*

A *Supreme* COMMAND

To have found God and

still to pursue Him is the

soul's paradox of love.

—*A. W. Tozer*

Contradiction

PRECIOUS
Pursuers

If you ever get so hungry

for God that you are in

pursuit of Him, He will do

things for you that He

won't do for anybody else.

—*Tommy Tenney*

The LORD would speak to

Moses face to face, as a

man speaks with his friend.

—*Exodus 33:11*

SYMPHONY OF *Prayer*

When the full measure of the
gathered prayers of God's people
finally reach a crescendoing echo in
God's ears, then it becomes too
much for Him to wait any longer.
He cannot pass by the prayers of
the brokenhearted and contrite
who seek His face. Finally the day
comes when God says from His
throne on high, "That's it."

—*Tommy Tenney*

THE KEY
TO
Self-discovery

If your first concern is to look

after yourself, you'll never find

yourself. But if you forget about

yourself and look to me, you'll

find both yourself and me.

—*Matthew 10:39* THE MESSAGE

Understand how the Father's

heart longs that His children

draw near to Him boldly. He

gave the blood of His Son to

secure it. Let us honour God, and

honour the blood, by entering

the Holiest with great boldness.

—*Andrew Murray*

Enter
IN **BOLDLY**

Moses longed for more than a visitation; his soul longed for habitation. He wanted more than just seeing God's finger or hearing His voice speaking from a cloud or a burning bush. He had gone beyond fear to love, and God's abiding presence had become his consuming desire.

—*Tommy Tenney*

Beyond FEAR

The interior journey of the soul

from the wilds of sin into the

enjoyed presence of God is

beautiful. Ransomed men need no

longer pause in fear to the Holy

of Holies. God wills that we

should push on into His presence

and live our whole life there.

—*A. W. Tozer*

PRESS *In*

If you make a habit of sincere prayer, your life will be very noticeably and profoundly altered. . . . Within the depths of consciousness, a flame kindles. And man sees himself. He discovers his selfishness, his silly pride, his fears, his greeds, his blunders. He develops a sense of moral obligation, intellectual humility. Thus begins a journey of the soul toward the realm of grace.

—*Alexis Carrel*

THE *Inner* LIFE

I love those who love me, and

those who seek me find me.

—*Proverbs 8:17*

Conversation

Tell God all that is in your heart, as one unloads one's heart, its pleasures and its pains, to a dear friend. Tell Him your troubles, that He may comfort you; tell Him your joys, that He may sober them; tell Him your longings, that He may purify them; tell Him your dislikes, that He may help you conquer them; talk to Him of your temptations, that He may shield you from them; show Him the wounds of your heart, that He may heal them; lay bare your indifference to good, your depraved tastes for evil, your instability. Tell Him how self-love makes you unjust to others, how vanity tempts you to be insincere, how pride disguises you to yourself and others.

If you thus pour out all your weaknesses, needs, troubles, there will be no lack of what to say. You will never exhaust the subject. It is continually being renewed. People who have no secrets from each other never want for subjects of conversation. They do not weigh their words, for there is nothing to be held back; neither do they seek for something to say. They talk out of the abundance of the heart, without consideration they say just what they think. Blessed are they who attain to such familiar, unreserved intercourse with God.

—*François Fénelon*

We must reject not only human cleverness, but also human prudence, which seems so important and so profitable. Then we may enter—like little children, with candor and innocence of worldly ways—into the simplicity of faith; and with humility and a horror of sin we may enter into the holy passion of the cross.

—*François Fénelon*

OUR *Holy* PASSION

We feel restless, frustrated, lonely in our spirits. We feel a greater need to have somebody with us, to protect us, shield us, wrap their arms around us, join us, walk with us. We soon discover that the presence of other people doesn't meet the need. The loneliness and restlessness we are feeling in our spirits is God's call to us. He is reeling us in to our one-on-one encounter with Him.

—*T. D. Jakes*

God
CALLING

ASPIRATIONS OF THE *Soul After* GOD

Transported I see thee display

Thy riches and glory divine;

I have only my life to repay,

Take what I would gladly resign.

Thy will is the treasure I seek,

For thou art as faithful as strong;

There let me, obedient and meek,

Repose myself all the day long.

My spirit and faculties fail;

Oh, finish what love has begun!

Destroy what is sinful and frail,

And dwell in the soul thou hast won!

Dear theme of my wonder and praise,

I cry, who is worthy as thou?

I can only be silent and gaze!

'Tis all that is left to me now.

—*Madame Jeanne Guyon*

God is calling you to a higher level of commitment. Forget the plans you've made for yourself and lie on His altar and die to self. Pray, "God, what do You want me to do?" It's time to lay everything aside and cover yourself in the blood. Nothing alive can stand in His presence. But if you're dead, then He will make you alive. So all you need to do is die if you really want to get into His presence. When the apostle Paul wrote, "I die daily," he was saying, "I enter into the presence of God every day."

—*Tommy Tenney*

(See 1 Corinthians 15:31.)

LIVING *Sacrifice*

SINGLE
Desire

Whom have I in heaven but

you? And earth has nothing I

desire besides you. My flesh

and my heart may fail, but

God is the strength of my

heart and my portion forever.

—*Psalm 73:25-26*

While we are looking at God, we do not see ourselves—blessed riddance. The man who has struggled to purify himself and has had nothing but repeated failures will experience real relief when he stops tinkering with his soul and looks away to the perfect One.

—*A. W. Tozer*

Shift YOUR FOCUS

THE *Call*

God is calling. The first time God revealed this to me, I trembled and wept in front of the people as I told them the same thing I tell you today: "You are at Mount Sinai today, and God is calling you into personal intimacy with Him. If you dare to answer His call, then it is going to redefine everything you've ever done." Your decision today will determine whether you go forward or backward in your walk with Christ.

—*Tommy Tenney*

RECOMMENDED *Reading* FOR THE HEART OF A GOD CHASER

God's Favorite House by Tommy Tenney

The God Chasers by Tommy Tenney

Confessions by Saint Augustine

On Loving God by Bernard of Clairvaux

The Image of the Heavenly by Jacob Boehme

Introduction to the Devout Life
   by Francis de Sales

*The Greatest Thing in the World and Other
   Addresses* by Henry Drummond

Religious Affections by Jonathan Edwards

Christian Perfection by François Fénelon

Spiritual Progress by François Fénelon

Experiencing the Depths of Jesus Christ
   by Madame Jeanne Guyon

The Dark Night of the Soul
   by Saint John of the Cross

Revelations of Divine Love
   by Julian of Norwich

Mere Christianity by C. S. Lewis

Why Revival Tarries by Leonard Ravenhill

The Divine Conquest by A.W. Tozer

The Pursuit of God by A.W. Tozer

The Cloud of Unknowing
    by an Anonymous Author

At the Master's Feet by Sadhu Sundar Singh

The Holiest of All by Andrew Murray

The Acceptable Sacrifice by John Bunyan

Digging the Wells of Revival by Lou Engle

The Imitation of Christ by Thomas à Kempis

A Serious Call to a Devout and Holy Life
    by William Law

The Practice of the Presence of God
    by Brother Lawrence

Many of the above titles are in the public domain and can be found in their entirety at the following websites:

Christian Classics Ethereal Library www.ccel.org
Internet Theology Resources: Spirituality
http://www.csbsju.edu/library/internet/theospir.html
JonathanEdwards.com
www.jonathanedwards.com
netLibrary.com
http://www.netlibrary.com/free_reading_room.asp
Dialogs and Documents from the Past
http://www.passtheword.org/DIALOGS-FROM-THE-PAST/

ABOUT
THE *Author*

Tommy Tenney is the author of the
best-selling books, *The God Chasers,
God's Dream Team,* and *God's Favorite
House.* He pastored for almost 10 years
and has spent more than 18 years as an
itinerant minister, sharing his passion
for the presence of God in more than 35
nations. He has experienced the
miraculous, but more importantly, he
knows the power of intimacy with and
humility before God. Tommy and his
wife Jeannie reside in Louisiana with
their three daughters, Tiffany, Natasha,
and Andrea.

OTHER
BOOKS BY
Tommy Tenney

The God Chasers
Published by Destiny Image

God's Favorite House
Published by Fresh Bread,
an imprint of Destiny Image

*The God Chaser's Daily Meditation and
Personal Journal*
Published by Destiny Image

God's Dream Team
Published by Regal, a division of Gospel Light

Secret Sources of Power
by T. F. Tenney and Tommy Tenney
Published by Destiny Image

God's Secret To Greatness
by Tommy Tenney and David Cape
Published by Regal, a division of Gospel Light

GodChasers.network is the ministry of Tommy
and Jeannie Tenney. Their heart's desire is to see the
presence and power of God fall—not just in
churches, but on cities and communities all over
the world.

HOW TO CONTACT US:

By Mail:

GodChasers.network
P.O. Box 3355
Pineville, Louisiana 71361
USA

By Phone:
   Voice: 318.44CHASE (318.442.4273)
   Fax: 318.442.6884
   Orders: 888.433.3355

By Internet:
E-mail: Contact@GodChasers.net
Website: www.GodChasers.net

JOIN TODAY

When you join the GodChasers.network we'll send you a free teaching tape!

If you share in our vision and want to stay current on how the Lord is using GodChasers.network, please add your name to our mailing list. We'd like to keep you updated on what the Spirit is saying through Tommy. We'll also send schedule updates and make you aware of new resources as they become available.

Sign up by calling or writing to (U.S. residents only):

Tommy Tenney
GodChasers.network
P.O. Box 3355
Pineville, Louisiana 71361-3355
USA

318-44CHASE (318.442.4273)

or sign up online at http://www.GodChasers.net/lists/

We regret that we are only able to send regular postal mailings to US residents at this time. If you live outside the US you can still add your postal address to our mailing list—you will automatically begin to receive our mailings as soon as they are available in your area.

E-mail Announcement List

If you'd like to receive information from us via e-mail, join our E-mail Announcement List by visiting our website at www.GodChasers.net/lists/.

"CHASE GOD" WITH US ONLINE!

The GodChasers.network is proud to bring you some of the most family-friendly Internet access available today! We've partnered with some Internet leaders to provide state-of-the art facilities, national dialup coverage, and 24-hour technical support. This is truly the best that the Internet has to offer: a service that is both reliable and safe! We use the industry's ONLY true artificial intelligence filter, the BAIR™ filtering System, so you can surf the net in a wholesome environment!

Features:

- Exclusive GodChasers.network Content
- Email address: Yourname@GodChasers.net
- Chat channels with opportunities to talk with Tommy and Jeannie Tenney, GodChasers staff, and guests
- Artificial Intelligence text and picture filtering
- Full Internet Capabilities
- Instant messaging
- Streaming audio/video
- Download MP3 Music files
- Much Much More!

For more information or to sign up today, you can visit our web site at http://www.GodChasers.com/. You can also call or write to us to receive software by mail!

AUDIOTAPE ALBUMS BY TOMMY TENNEY

P.O. Box 3355
Pineville, Louisiana 71361-3355
318.44CHASE (318.442.4273)

FANNING THE FLAMES
(audiotape album) $20 plus $4.50 S&H

Tape 1 — The Application of the Blood and the Ark of the Covenant: Jesus made atonement with His own blood, once for all, and the veil in the temple was rent from top to bottom.

Tape 2 — A Tale of Two Cities—Nazareth & Nineveh: Jesus spent more time in Nazareth than any other city, yet there was great resistance to the works of God there.

Tape 3 — The "I" Factor: Examine the difference between *ikabod* and *kabod* ("glory"). The arm of flesh cannot achieve what needs to be done. God doesn't need us; we need Him.

KEYS TO LIVING THE REVIVED LIFE
(audiotape album) $20 plus $4.50 S&H

Tape 1 - Fear Not: The principles that Tommy reveals teach us that to have no fear is to have faith, and that perfect love casts out fear, so we establish the trust of a child in our loving Father.

Tape 2 - Hanging in There: Have you ever been tempted to give up, quit, and throw in the towel? This message is a word of encouragement for you. Everybody has a place and a position in the Kingdom of God.

Tape 3 - Fire of God: Fire purges the sewer of our souls and destroys the hidden things that would cause disease. Learn the way out of a repetitive cycle of seasonal times of failure.

NEW! GOD'S DREAM TEAM AUDIO SERIES
(audiotape album) $20 plus $4.50 S&H

Only we can answer the only unanswered prayer of Jesus. "That they may be one!" This collection contains three of Tommy's messages on unity.

Additional copies of this book and other book
titles from ALBURY PUBLISHING are available at your
local bookstore.

ALBURY PUBLISHING
P. O. Box 470406
Tulsa, Oklahoma 74147-0406

For a complete list of our titles, visit us at our
website: www.alburypublishing.com

For international and Canadian orders,
please contact:

Access Sales International
2448 East 81st Street
Suite 4900
Tulsa, Oklahoma 74137

Phone 918-523-5590

Fax 918-496-2822